French verbs simplified : rules for the formation of tenses, and complete tables for reference, showing at a glance the conjugation of every verb, regular or irregular

Hugo's Language Institute

HUGO'S

FRENCH in 3 Months

WITHOUT A MASTER

Set of three separate volumes in paper covers.

I.—A SIMPLE BUT COMPLETE GRAMMAR, containing all the rules necessary for speaking and writing French correctly.

II.—FRENCH PRONUNCIATION ; a series of Easy Anecdotes, with the Translation and Pronunciation of every word.

III.—A KEY to the Conversational Exercises in the Grammar.

In all 184 pages **3/-** complete.

HUGO'S

FRENCH SIMPLIFIED

Similar to the above but contains an extra part, FRENCH IDIOMS. This section consists of practical sentences, introducing all the important Idioms and peculiarities of French construction.

280 pages, cloth **5/-** *complete in one vol.*

HUGO'S

SPANISH in 3 Months

WITHOUT A MASTER

Set of three separate volumes in paper covers.

I.—A SIMPLE BUT COMPLETE GRAMMAR, containing all the rules necessary for speaking and writing Spanish correctly.

II.—SPANISH CONVERSATION : Miscellaneous Conversational Sentences, introducing all the important idioms, etc.

III.—A KEY to the Conversational Exercises in the Grammar.

In all 176 pages **3/-** complete.

HUGO'S
SPANISH SIMPLIFIED

Similar to the above but contains an extra part, SPANISH READING : A collection of amusing and interesting anecdotes and dialogues. etc., carefully selected and copiously annotated.

240 pages, cloth **5/-** *complete in one vol.*

*FLEMISH can also be learnt by this book.

Hugo's SWEDISH SIMPLIFIED

Complete in 2 parts (not sold separately), 160 pp., **3s.** net.

A practical guide to modern conversational Swedish. Compiled throughout on Hugo's well known Simplified System. Contains a Condensed and Simplified Grammar, Practical Conversation, Graduated Reading Exercises, consisting of Easy Anecdotes, Short Stories, etc., Lists of Regular and Irregular Verbs, Commercial Phrases, Indispensable Words, etc.

☞ IMITATED PRONUNCIATION OF EVERY WORD.

HUGO'S DANISH SIMPLIFIED

Complete in 2 parts (not sold separately), 160 pp., **3s.** net.

Although there is a great similarity between the Languages of Denmark and Norway, they are nevertheless each distinct from the other, especially as regards the pronunciation. This is exclusively a Danish text-book and consequently is free from the defects which are bound to be present in any attempt to deal with the two languages together. It is the most thoroughly practical guide obtainable to modern conversational Danish.

IMITATED PRONUNCIATION THROUGHOUT.

HUGO'S
NORWEGIAN SIMPLIFIED

Complete in 2 parts (not sold separately), 160 pp., **3s.** net.

Exclusively a Norwegian text-book, and is the only book by which a really practical knowledge of the language can be acquired.

IMITATED PRONUNCIATION OF EVERY WORD.

FOREIGN BUSINESS CORRESPONDENCE

HUGO'S publish a series of books of great value to all who are likely to have much to do with Foreign Business Correspondence. These books not only show the student how to construct various kinds of business letters, but also familiarise him with expressions likely to be met with in letters received from the respective countries.

FRENCH COMMERCIAL CORRESPONDENT
312 pages, cloth ... **5/-** net

SPANISH COMMERCIAL CORRESPONDENT
192 pages, cloth ... **3/6** net

GERMAN COMMERCIAL CORRESPONDENT
192 pages, cloth ... **3/6** net

ITALIAN COMMERCIAL CORRESPONDENT
192 pages, cloth ... **3/6** net

Hugo's VERBS SIMPLIFIED

A Series of Books which will elucidate every difficulty in connection with this subject. The Student is no longer burdened with a tremendous amount of memorising ; a few important rules save much of this needless labour.

FRENCH VERBS SIMPLIFIED, cloth, **2s.** net.

SPANISH VERBS SIMPLIFIED, cloth, **2s.** net.

ITALIAN VERBS SIMPLIFIED, cloth, **2s.** net.

GERMAN VERBS SIMPLIFIED, cloth, **2s.** net.

HUGO'S SIMPLIFIED SYSTEM.

FRENCH VERBS SIMPLIFIED.

RULES FOR THE FORMATION OF TENSES;

AND

COMPLETE TABLES FOR REFERENCE,

SHOWING AT A GLANCE

THE CONJUGATION OF EVERY VERB,

Regular and Irregular.

PUBLISHED BY

HUGO'S LANGUAGE INSTITUTE,

103 NEWGATE STREET, LONDON, E.C. 1; and Branches.

PREFACE.

This work forms one of "HUGO'S SIMPLIFIED SERIES." the chief object of which is to save the Student's time by giving no Rules but those actually necessary. In this case, however, as with "FRENCH GENDERS SIMPLIFIED," the greater part of the book is *for Reference only.* The tables appended, which may be taken out and mounted, will be found specially convenient for reference, as they show at a glance every Number, Person, Mood, and Tense of *every Verb*, Regular or Irregular.

Students should first learn the regular terminations (see page 6), referring to the Rules on the Formation of Tenses opposite. This is quickly done by taking one Tense at a time, the best order to follow being **Present, Perfect, Future, Imperfect, Conditional**, etc, as laid down in HUGO'S "FRENCH GRAMMAR SIMPLIFIED."

When the Regular Verbs have been thoroughly mastered, the **Irregular Verbs** present no difficulty. All that need be learnt is the irregularities of important Verbs, which are indicated by **thick type.**

No English for the Subjunctive Mood should be learned The translation usually given,—"that I may speak," or "might speak," is most misleading, and often absolutely wrong. The only safe way is to learn when to employ this Mood.

We omit *que* before the French Subjunctive, as it is no part of this Mood, and neither always precedes it nor always governs it It is advisable, however, to insert it in replies to examination questions.

Fuller conjugations of the *Compound Tenses*, and of the *Negative* and *Interrogative Forms*, are omitted, as they require no learning whatever. The mere sight of these as given in most Grammars appals and disheartens the Student, and the formation is precisely the *same throughout every Verb* in the language

For the same reason, we give no list of the Verbs requiring "de" before a following Infinitive. There is no occasion to learn these Verbs, if it is borne in mind that *all Verbs* require "de" unless given in our Lists of those requiring "à," or no Preposition.

We believe that this work will be found a great help to the beginner who has not yet mastered the Verbs, and an invaluable book of reference for the advanced Student.

CONTENTS.

TABLES FOR REFERENCE.
(To be found in pocket at end of book.)

A.) **Complete Conjugation of the Regular and Auxiliary Verbs.**

B.) **Complete List of the Irregular Verbs.**

C.) **Complete Conjugation of every Irregular Verb,** arranged so that any Mood, Tense, Number, or Person, can be ascertained at a glance.

THE FRENCH VERBS.

The Verb is the most important part of Speech in all languages, and should therefore be learned thoroughly.

Verbs are divided into two classes,—*Transitive* and *Intransitive*.

Transitive Verbs are so called because they transmit the action from the *Subject* to the *Object*; as,

I (*Subject*) buy (*Verb*) a house (*Object*).

Verbs consist of *Voices, Moods, Tenses, Numbers* and *Persons*.

There are two Voices, the *Active Voice* and the *Passive Voice*.

In the *Active Voice* the Subject of the Verb is the *doer* of the action expressed; as,

the boy (*Subject*) plays (*Verb*).

The Active Voice often expresses a state or condition, as the boy sleeps.

In the *Passive Voice* the Subject of the Verb is the *receiver* of the action expressed; as,

the boy (*Subject*) is beaten (*Verb*).

There are five Moods, viz:

1, *Infinitive*, 2, *Indicative*, 3, *Subjunctive*, 4, *Imperative*, 5, *Conditional*.

The Principal Tenses are ·

Present, *Past*, and *Future*, supplemented by Auxiliary Tenses, as shown in the *Model Conjugation* of an English Verb.

There are three Persons, each having two Numbers, the *Singular* and the *Plural*; as,

	Sing.	Plur.			Sing.	Plur
1st Person	I	we	3rd Person	masc.	he	}
2nd „	thou	you		fem.	she	} they
				neut.	it	}

TRANSITIVE VERBS,

or Active Verbs, as they are sometimes called, require an *Object* to complete the sense. For instance:

I find conveys no complete meaning; but, *I find the* **book**, *he found the* **street**, etc , are complete sentences.

INTRANSITIVE VERBS,

or Neuter Verbs as they are sometimes called, convey a complete meaning without the addition of an *Object*.

Examples. *I sang, he reads, they slept,* etc.

Intransitive Verbs can occasionally be employed as Transitive; as,—*I sang a* **song**, *he reads a* **book**, etc.

The Objects in the foregoing examples are indicated by thick type.

IMPERSONAL or UNIPERSONAL VERBS

can only be used in the third person Singular; as,

it is thundering, it was snowing, it will rain.

TERMINATIONS OF THE REGULAR CONJUGATIONS.

(see General Rules on the formation of Tenses)

The following terminations are added to the *Stem* in all Tenses except the *Future* and *Conditional*; in these two they are added to the *Infinitive*.

1. INFINITIVE.

parl-er vend-re fin-ir

2. PRESENT PARTICIPLE.

er	parl-	
re	vend-	}ant
ir	finiss-	

3. PAST PARTICIPLE.

er	parl-é
re	vend-u
ir	fin-i

INDICATIVE

4. PRESENT TENSE.

		je	*tu*	*il*	*nous*	*vous*	*ils*
er	parl-	e	es	e			
re	vend-	s	s	—	}ons	ez	ent
ir	fin-	is	is	it			
		Plural Stem. finiss-					

5 FUTURE

		je	*tu*	*il*	*nous*	*vous*	*ils*
er	parler-						
re	vendr(e)-	}ai	as	a	ons	ez	ont
ir	finir-						

6. CONDITIONAL

er	parler-						
re	vendr(e)-	}ais	ais	ait	ions	iez	aient
ir	finir-						

7. IMPERFECT *or* PAST.

er	parl-						
re	vend-	}ais	ais	ait	ions	iez	aient
ir	finiss-						

8. PAST DEFINITE *or* PRETERITE.

er	parl-	ai	as	a	âmes	âtes	èrent
re	vend-	}is	is	it	îmes	îtes	irent
ir	fin-						

SUBJUNCTIVE.

9. PRESENT.

er	parl-						
re	vend-	}e	es	e	ions	iez	ent
ir	finiss-						

10. IMPERFECT *or* PAST.

er	parl-	asse	asses	ât	assions	assiez	assent
re	vend-	}isse	isses	ît	issions	issiez	issent
ir	fin-						

11. IMPERATIVE.

		SING *2nd person.*	PLUR · *1st person.*	*2nd person*
er	parl-	e	ons	ez
re	vend-	s	ons	ez
ir	fin-	is	issons	issez

GENERAL RULES ON THE FORMATION OF TENSES.

1. The Infinitive of all Regular French Verbs ends in er, re, or ir. The *Stem* is the part of the verb which precedes *er*, *re*, or *ir*.

2. As shown by the terminations opposite, the *Present Participle* is formed by adding *ant* to the *Stem* of all verbs; verbs in *ir* prefix *iss* to the *ant*; as,—*parlant, vendant, finissant*.

3. The *Past Participle* of verbs ending in *er* is pronounced like the *Infinitive*.

4. The terminations, added in the *Singular* of the *Present* of verbs in *er* and *re*, are not pronounced. The Plural terminations of all verbs are *ons*, *ez*, *ent* (this *ent* is always mute); verbs in *ir* prefix *iss* to the Plural terminations.

5. The terminations of the *Future* are the same as those of *j'ai, tu as, il a*, etc. They are added to the *Infinitive*, the *e* of verbs in *re* being omitted, as,—*je parlerai, il vendra, nous finirons*.

6. The Conditional is formed by adding the terminations to the *Infinitive*, the *e* of verbs in *re* being omitted; as,
je parlerais, il vendrait, nous finirions.

7. The terminations of the Imperfect are the same as those of the Conditional; but they are added to the *Stem* (not to the Infinitive). Verbs in *ir* prefix *iss* to these terminations throughout the tense; as,
je parlais, nous vendions, il finissait.

8. The terminations of the Singular in the Past Definite of verbs in *er* are the same as those of *j'ai, tu as, il a*; and of verbs in *re* and *ir* the same as those of the *Present* of verbs in *ir*; as,
je parlai, tu parlas, il parla, je vendis, tu vendis, il vendit; je finis, tu finis, il finit.

The Plural of the Past Definite only differs in the Vowel:

Verbs in $\left\{ \begin{array}{l} er \\ re \ \& \ ir \end{array} \right\}$ $\left. \begin{array}{l} \hat{a} \\ \hat{i} \end{array} \right\}$ mes $\left. \begin{array}{l} \hat{a} \\ \hat{i} \end{array} \right\}$ tes $\left. \begin{array}{l} \grave{e} \\ i \end{array} \right\}$ rent

9. The terminations of the Present Subjunctive are the same as those of *the Present Indicative of verbs ending in* er, an i being prefixed to *ons* and *ez*. Verbs in *ir* prefix *iss* to the terminations throughout the tense; as,
il parle, nous parlions, tu vendes, vous vendiez, je finisse, nous finissions, ils finissent

10. The Imperfect Subjunctive is the same as *the Present Subjunctive of verbs in* ir (*je finisse*, etc.), except in the 3rd person singular, where *isse* is changed to *ît*. Verbs in *er*, however, substitute *a* for *i* throughout the tense, as,
je parlasse, il parlât, vous parlassiez, tu vendisses, il vendît, je finisse, tu finisses, il finît, nous finissions, ils finissent

11. The Imperative has really only three persons; viz. 2nd person Singular, and 1st & 2nd person Plural

These persons are formed by omitting the pronouns *tu, nous, vous* from the Present of the Indicative. Verbs in *er* elide the *s* in the 2nd person Singular.

The forms for the 3rd person, *let him speak* and *let them speak*, are simply the 3rd person of the *Present Subjunctive* with *que* prefixed; as,—let him sell *qu'il vende*, let them finish *qu'ils finissent*.

HINTS ON THE FORMATION OF THE AUXILIARY VERBS

The Future of *avoir* is formed by adding the terminations *ai, as, a, ons, ez, ont,* to aur, and of *être* by adding them to ser; as,

j'aurai, tu auras, il aura, etc. *je serai, tu seras, il sera*, etc.

The Conditional of *avoir* is formed by adding the terminations *ais, ais, ait, ions, iez, aient,* to aur and of *être* by adding them to ser; as,

j'aurais, tu aurais, il aurait, etc. *je serais, tu serais, il serait,* etc.

The Imperfect of *avoir* is formed by adding the terminations *ais, ais, ait, ions, iez, aient,* to av, and of *être* by adding them to et; as,

j'avais, il avait, nous avions, etc. *j'étais, vous étiez, ils étaient,* etc.

The Past Definite of *avoir* is *j'eus, tu eus, il eut, nous eûmes, vous eûtes, ils eurent.* The Past Definite of *être* can be formed by changing the *e* of the above into *f* —*je fus, tu fus, il fut, nous fûmes, vous fûtes, ils furent.*

The Present Subjunctive of *avoir* and *être* is very irregular, and must therefore be learned by heart.

The Imperative of *avoir* and *être* is the same as the Present of the Subjunctive, the Pronouns *tu, vous, nous,* being omitted; thus:

have *aie(s), ayez;* let us have *ayons*
be *sois, soyez;* let us be *soyons*

For the forms: let him have *qu'il ait,* let them have *qu'ils aient,* see No. 11, General Rules on the Formation of Tenses

---

LIST OF REGULAR VERBS SUITABLE FOR CONJUGATION AS PRACTICE.

VERBS IN er.

to accept *accepter*	to think *penser*	to pass *passer*
to sing *chanter*	to play *jouer*	to accompany *accompagner*
to hide *cacher*	to turn *tourner*	
to copy *copier*	to study *étudier*	to show *montrer*
to give *donner*	to forget *oublier*	to mount *monter*
to knock, strike *frapper*	to find *trouver*	to breakfast *déjeuner*
	to visit *visiter*	

VERBS IN re.

to wait for *attendre*	to sell *rendre*	to bite *mordre*
to descend *descendre*	to hold out *tendre*	to lose *perdre*
to hear *entendre*	to correspond *correspondre*	to defend *défendre*
to hang *pendre*		to reply *répondre*

VERBS IN ir.

to punish *punir*	to fill *remplir*	to succeed *réussir*
to obey *obéir*	to accomplish *accomplir*	to grow pale *pâlir*
to choose *choisir*	to build *bâtir*	to furnish *fournir*

THE COMPOUND TENSES

are formed as in English with the *Past Participle* and the auxiliary verb *avoir*, to have, and therefore do not require any study.

For Compound Tenses formed with "être," to be, see Passive Voice.

List of Compound Tenses for Reference.

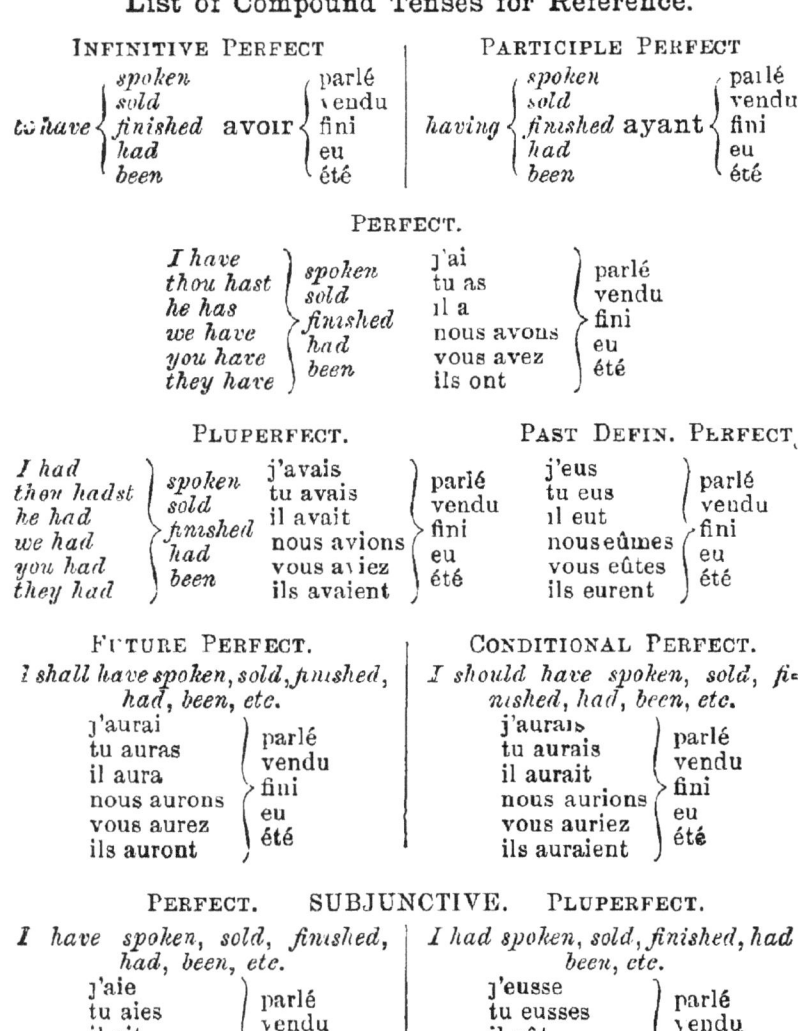

INFINITIVE PERFECT

to have { *spoken, sold, finished, had, been* } avoir { parlé, vendu, fini, eu, été }

PARTICIPLE PERFECT

having { *spoken, sold, finished, had, been* } ayant { parlé, vendu, fini, eu, été }

PERFECT.

I have, thou hast, he has, we have, you have, they have { *spoken, sold, finished, had, been* }

j'ai, tu as, il a, nous avons, vous avez, ils ont { parlé, vendu, fini, eu, été }

PLUPERFECT.

I had, thou hadst, he had, we had, you had, they had { *spoken, sold, finished, had, been* }

j'avais, tu avais, il avait, nous avions, vous aviez, ils avaient { parlé, vendu, fini, eu, été }

PAST DEFIN. PERFECT.

j'eus, tu eus, il eut, nouseûmes, vous eûtes, ils eurent { parlé, vendu, fini, eu, été }

FUTURE PERFECT.

I shall have spoken, sold, finished, had, been, etc.

j'aurai, tu auras, il aura, nous aurons, vous aurez, ils auront { parlé, vendu, fini, eu, été }

CONDITIONAL PERFECT.

I should have spoken, sold, finished, had, been, etc.

j'aurais, tu aurais, il aurait, nous aurions, vous auriez, ils auraient { parlé, vendu, fini, eu, été }

PERFECT.   SUBJUNCTIVE.   PLUPERFECT.

I have spoken, sold, finished, had, been, etc.

j'aie, tu aies, il ait, nous ayons, vous ayez, ils aient { parlé, vendu, fini, eu, été }

I had spoken, sold, finished, had, been, etc.

j'eusse, tu eusses, il eût, nous eussions, vous eussiez, ils eussent { parlé, vendu, fini, eu, été }

F. V. 2.

THE INTERROGATIVE FORM.

Questions are formed in French by placing the Pronouns after the Verb ; the Verb and Pronoun are connected by a hyphen (-); as,

I have *j'ai*	Question : have I ? *ai-je ?*
he is *il est*	., is he ? *est-il ?*

MODEL TENSE IN INTERROGATIVE FORM.

have I ? *ai-je ?*	have we ? *avons-nous ?*
hast thou ? *as-tu ?*	have you ? *avez-vous ?*
has he ? *a-t-il ?*	have they ? *ont-ils ?*

The words *do, does, did,* which are used in questions in English, are not translated in French ; as,

do you speak ? = speak you ? *parlez-vous ?*
does she sell ? = sells she ? *vend-elle ?*

If the Verb ends in a vowel in the 3rd person singular, a *t* between two hyphens (-*t*-) is put in questions between the Verb and the Pronoun ; as,

has he ? *a-t-il ?*	does he speak ? *parle-t-il ?*
will she be ? *sera-t-elle ?*	did he speak ? *parla-t-il ?*

———— o ————

THE NEGATIVE FORM.

Negations are formed in French by two words *ne...pas*, NOT ; *ne* is put before the Verb and *pas* after it ; as,

I am not *je ne suis pas* , are they not ? *ne sont-ils pas ?*

ne before a vowel becomes *n'* ; as,

I have not *je n'ai pas* : have you not ? *n'avez-vous pas ?*

MODEL TENSE IN NEGATIVE FORM.

I was not *je n'étais pas*	we were not *nous n'étions pas*
thou wast not *tu n'étais pas*	you were not *vous n'étiez pas*
he was not *il n'était pas*	they were not *ils n'étaient pas*

MODEL TENSE IN NEGATIVE INTERROGATIVE FORM.

am I not ? *ne suis-je pas ?*	are we not ? *ne sommes-nous pas ?*
art thou not ? *n'es-tu pas ?*	are you not ? *n'êtes-vous pas ?*
is he not ? *n'est-il pas ?*	are they not ? *ne sont-ils pas ?*

do, does, did, are not translated ; as,

I do not speak *je ne parle pas* ; does he not speak ? *ne parle-t-il pas ?*
we did not speak *nous ne parlions pas, nous n'avons pas parlé*

pas is put after the *Auxiliary* in Compound Tenses, as in English ; as,

I have not spoken	*have I not spoken?*
je n'ai pas parlé	n'ai-je pas parlé ?
tu n'as pas parlé	n'as-tu pas parlé ?
il n'a pas parlé, etc.	n'a-t-il pas parlé ? etc.

EXPLANATION AND USE OF TENSES.

(See Model Conjugation of English Verb at end.)

1. The Present Tense is employed as in English, but it has only one form in French ; and thus the English Progressive form, *I am speaking*, etc., has no equivalent in French, but must be translated like *I speak*, etc.

Thus change when translating :

I am speaking *into* I speak	we are speaking *into* we speak
thou art „ „ thou speakest	you are „ „ you „
he(she)is „ „ he(she)speaks	they are „ „ they „

Questions are formed in all French verbs by putting the *pronoun* after the *verb* ; *do* and *does* are not translated.

Thus change when translating :

do I speak	*or*	am I speaking	*into*	speak I ?
dost thou speak	„	art thou „	„	speakest thou ?
does he(she) „	„	is he(she) „	„	speaks he (she)?
do we	„	„	are we „	„	speak we ?
do you	„	„	are you ,	„	speak you?
do they	„	„	are they „	„	speak they ?

The *Negation* of all Verbs in French is formed alike.

Thus change when translating :

I do not speak	*or* I am not speaking *into* I speak not
thou dost not speak	„ thou art not „	„ thou speakest not
he does „ „	„ he is „ „	„ he speaks „
we do „ „	„ we are „ „	„ we speak „
you do „ „	„ you are „ „	„ you „ „
they do „ „	„ they are „ „	„ they „ „

(*Interrogative Negative Form.*)

do I not speak	*or* am I not speaking *into* speak I not?
dost thou not speak	„ art thou not „	„ speakest thou not?
does he „ „	„ is he „ „	„ speaks he „
do we „ „	„ are we „ „	„ speak we „
do you „ „	„ are you „ „	„ speak you „
do they „ „	„ are they „ „	„ speak they „

2. The Perfect Tense, formed with the *past participle* and the auxiliary *to have* (sometimes *to be*), is generally employed in French instead of the English *past* or *imperfect tense* ; thus translate :

I spoke	*by*	I have spoken	*j'ai parlé*
he lost	„	he has lost	*il a perdu*
we finished	„	we have finished	*nous avons fini*

The word **did**, used in English Questions and Negations, must be changed into *has* or *have*, as,

did he speak	=	*has* he spoken	*a-t-il parlé?*
I did not lose	=	I *have* not lost	*je n'ai pas perdu*
did you finish	=	*have* you finished	*avez-vous fini?*
did they not speak	=	*have* they not spoken	*n'ont-ils pas parlé?*

The English Progressive form is also translated by the Perfect; thus,

I have been speaking	=	I have spoken
has he not been „	=	has he not spoken

3. THE IMPERFECT TENSE in French must be employed, if in English the Progressive form *I was speaking, etc.* is used, or if *I spoke* has the meaning of *I was speaking* or *I used to speak.*

Questions and Negations with *did* must also be translated by the *Imperfect*, if the English can be changed into the *progressive form* without altering the sense; thus,

Did you speak must be translated by *parliez-vous* if it has the meaning of *were you speaking* or *used you to speak?*

She did not finish must be translated by *elle ne finissait pas* if it has the meaning of *she was not finishing* or *she used not to finish.*

The expressions *I used to speak* or *I was in the habit of speaking*, are simply translated by the French Imperfect *je parlais*

Thus change when translating:

I was speaking	or	I used to speak	=	I spoke	
we were „	„	we used to „	=	we spoke	
I was not speaking	or	I did not speak	=	I spoke not	
you were not „	,	you did not „	=	you spoke not	
was I speaking	or	did I speak	=	spoke I	
were they „	„	did they „	=	spoke they	
was I not „	..	did I not „	=	spoke I not	
was he not „	..	did he not „	=	spoke he not	

4. The PAST DEFINITE is used in translating the English PAST TENSE, when the incident referred to has taken place at a time completely gone by.

This tense, which is sometimes called the HISTORIC PAST, chiefly occurs in *written* narration, and is very rarely employed in conversation.

5. The FUTURE and CONDITIONAL are employed as in English, but they, like all the other tenses, have no progressive form.

Thus change when translating :

I shall be speaking	=	I shall speak
he will not be ,,	=	he will not speak
shall we be ,,	=	shall we speak
will you not be ,,	=	will you not speak
I should be speaking	=	I should speak
would you not be ,,	=	would you not speak
I had been speaking	=	I had spoken

Be careful to note that the English Future Auxiliaries are *shall* for the first person, and *will* for the other persons. In the Conditional *should* is the Auxiliary for the first person, and *would* for the other persons. If this distinction is not observed, the meaning is entirely altered. For example, *I* **shall** *go to-morrow, and he* **will** *come too*, simply expresses futurity; but in the sentence *I* **will** *go to-morrow, and he* **shall** *come too*, *will* implies intention, and *shall* compulsion.

6. The IMPERATIVE MOOD is used as in English.

7. The SUBJUNCTIVE MOOD is employed in DEPENDENT CLAUSES, after Verbs expressing *doubt, will, wish, necessity, fear*, etc. Some Conjunctions, the most important of which are given in Lesson 26 of our French Grammar, always require the following Verb to be in the Subjunctive.

REMARKS ON VERBS ENDING IN oir.

There are seven Verbs ending in ev*oir*, all of which are conjugated alike. They are : *devoir* to owe, *recevoir* to receive, *concevoir* to conceive, *décevoir* to deceive, *redevoir* to owe again, *apercevoir* to perceive, and *percevoir* to collect money (taxes). These seven Verbs are generally classified as regular, the conjugations being arranged in the following order :

1st Conjugation,	Verbs	ending	in	*er*
2nd	,,	,,	,,	*ir*
3rd	,,	,,	,,	*oir*
4th	,,	,,	,,	*re*

14

All Verbs, however, which end in *oir*, not in **evoir**, are quite irregular, and some of the best modern grammarians classify those in *evoir* as irregular also. This arrangement we have adopted, as there are many groups, especially those ending in *indre* and *uire*, which, although nearly always classified as irregular, are more numerous and important than the Verbs in *evoir*. *Devoir*, *recevoir*, and *apercevoir*, are the only three which are in common use.

THE REFLECTIVE VERBS.

A Transitive Verb (for explanation of *transitive*, see beginning) becomes *reflective* in English if followed by one of the Reflective Pronouns *myself, himself, etc.*; as,

NOT REFLECTIVE: I am warming the room
REFLECTIVE: I am warming *myself*
NOT REFLECTIVE: He is amusing the children
REFLECTIVE: He is amusing *himself*

The REFLECTIVE PRONOUNS are the same as the ordinary Objective Pronouns, thus:

myself **me** ourselves **nous**
thyself **te** yourself, yourselves **vous**
except, himself, herself, itself, themselves, one's self } which are translated **se**

EXAMPLE OF A VERB CONJUGATED REFLECTIVELY.

to wash one's self **se laver.**

PRESENT

I wash myself	*je me lave*
thou washest thyself	*tu te laves*
he washes himself	*il se lave*
she washes herself	*elle se lave*
we wash ourselves	*nous nous lavons*
you wash yourself, yourselves	*vous vous lavez*
they wash themselves	*ils se lavent*
they (*f.*) wash themselves	*elles se lavent*

Imperfect.	I was washing myself	*je me lavais, etc.*
Future:	I shall wash myself	*je me laverai, etc.*
Conditional.	I should wash myself	*je me laverais, etc.*
Imperative:	wash yourself	*lavez-vous*
	do not wash yourself	*ne vous lavez pas*
	let us wash ourselves	*lavons-nous*

The Compound Tenses of all Reflective Verbs are formed with *être*, and thus the Past Participle takes the gender and number of the Subject ; as,

PERFECT.

I have washed myself	*je me suis lavé(e)*
thou hast washed thyself	*tu t'es lavé(e)*
he has washed himself	*il s'est lavé*
she has washed herself	*elle s'est lavée*
we have washed ourselves	*nous nous sommes lavés(es)*
you have washed yourself	*vous vous êtes lavé(e)*
you have washed yourselves	*vous vous êtes lavés(es)*
they have washed themselves	*ils se sont lavés*
they (*f.*) have washed themselves	*elles se sont lavées*

I have not washed myself	*je ne me suis pas lavé*
has he washed himself?	*s'est-il lavé ?*

I had washed myself	*je m'étais lavé, etc.*
I shall have washed myself	*je me serai lavé, etc.*
I should have washed myself	*je me serais lavé, etc.*

There are a great many verbs which are *reflective* in French, but not in English ; as,

to make a mistake se tromper

I make a mistake	*je me trompe*
thou makest a mistake	*tu te trompes*
he makes a mistake	*il se trompe*
we make a mistake	*nous nous trompons*
you make a mistake	*vous vous trompez*
they make a mistake	*ils se trompent*

I was making a mistake *je me trompais*
I have made a mistake *je me suis trompé* (fem . *trompée*)
we have made a mistake *nous nous sommes trompés* (fem *trompées*)
do not make a mistake *ne vous trompez pas*

The Compound Tenses of the following verbs are always formed with *être*.

aller *to go*	devenir *to become*
sortir *to go out*	arriver *to arrive*
partir *to go away, to set out*	entrer *to enter*
venir *to come*	rester *to remain, to stay*
revenir *to come back*	tomber *to fall*

EXAMPLE.

Past Tense.		Perfect Tense.	
I went	*or* I have gone		*je suis allé (allée)*
thou wentest	,, thou hast gone		*tu es allé (allée)*
he went	,, he has gone		*il est allé*
she went	,, she has gone		*elle est allée*
we went	., we have gone		*nous sommes allés (allées)*
you went	,, you have gone		*vous êtes allé(e) (allé(e)s)*
they went	., they have gone		*ils sont allés*
they (f) went	,, they (f) have gone		*elles sont allées*

If **you** is masculine singular use *allé*, if feminine singular use *allée*, if masculine plural *allés*, and if feminine plural *allées*

SOME REFLECTIVE VERBS FOR PRACTICE.

to be *se porter*
to exclaim *s'écrier*
to rest *se reposer*
to complain *se plaindre*
to repent *se repentir*
to take a walk *se pro-mener*
to get up *se lever*
to make haste *se dé-pêcher*
to repair to *se rendre*
to recollect *se souvenir*

THE PASSIVE VOICE.

The Passive Voice is formed as in English, with the *Past Participle* and the auxiliary verb *être*, to be.

The Passive Voice is not much used in French.

The *Past Participle*, after the verb *être*, agrees in gender and number with its Subject, like an Adjective.

PRESENT OF THE INDICATIVE

I am honoured	*je suis honoré*, fem *honorée*
thou art honoured	*tu es honoré*, fem: *honorée*
he is honoured	*il est honoré*
she is honoured	*elle est honorée*
we are honoured	*nous sommes honorés*, fem *honorées*
you are honoured SING.	*vous êtes honoré*, fem. *honorée*
you are honoured PLUR.	*vous êtes honorés*, fem *honorées*
they are honoured MASC.	*ils sont honorés*
they are honoured FEM.	*elles sont honorées*

IMPERFECT.

I was honoured   *j'étais honoré*
she was honoured   *elle était honorée*

PAST DEFINITE.

was honoured *je fus honoré*

FUTURE.

I shall be honoured   *je serai honoré*
we shall be honoured   *nous serons honorés*

CONDITIONAL.

I should be honoured   *je serais honoré*
we should be honoured   *nous serions honorés*

PERFECT.

I have been honoured *j'ai été honoré*

INFINITIVE.

to be honoured *être honoré*

PRESENT PARTICIPLE.

being honoured *étant honoré*

PECULIARITIES OF VERBS ENDING IN er.

Verbs ending in **ger** or **cer** change *g* into *ge*, and *c* into *ç* cedilla before a termination commencing with *a* or *o*.

This is done to preserve the soft sound of the *g* or *c* of the Infinitive.

EXAMPLES : to judge *juger*	to commence *commencer*
we judge *nous jugeons*	we commence *nous commençons*

Most verbs ending in **eler** or **eter** double the *l* or *t* when it is followed by an *e* mute.

e is always mute except in the terminations *ez* and *er*.

EXAMPLES :—to spell *épeler* ,	to throw *jeter*
I spell *j'épelle*	we spell *nous epelons*
thou spellest *tu épelles*	you spell *vous épelez*
he spells *il epelle*	they spell *ils épellent*

I shall spell *j'épellerai,* etc

I throw *je jette*	we throw *nous jetons*
thou throwest *tu jettes*	you throw *vous jetez*
he throws *il jette*	they throw *ils jettent*

I shall throw *je jetterai,* etc.

The following verbs do not double the *l* or *t*, but change the first *e* into *è*, if the *l* or *t* is followed by an *e* mute.

acheter to buy, *bourreler* to torment, *congeler* to congeal, *déceler* to disclose, dégeler to thaw, geler to freeze, *harceler* to harass, peler to peel, *colleter* to collar, *décolleter* to bare one's neck and shoulders, *étiqueter* to label, *trompeter* to trumpet, *coqueter* to coquet

EXAMPLE · *I buy,* j'achète, tu achètes, il achète ,
nous achetons, vous achetez, ils achètent.

I was buying, j'achetais, etc.

I shall buy, j'achèterai, tu achèteras, il achètera , nous achèterons, etc

Verbs ending in *er*, preceded by *e* and a consonant, change the *e* into *è* if the termination begins with *e* mute (i.e , before *e*, *es*, or *ent*).

EXAMPLE   to lead **mener**
I lead, je mène, tu mènes, il mène ;
nous menons, vous menez, ils mènent.
I was leading, je menais, *etc.*
I shall lead, je mènerai, tu mèneras, *etc.*

Verbs ending in *er*, preceded by *é* and a consonant, undergo the same change, except in the Future and Conditional.

EXAMPLE :—to hope **espérer**
I hope, j'espère, tu espères, il espère ;
nous espérons, vous espérez, ils espèrent
I was hoping, j'espérais, *etc.*
I shall hope, j'espérerai, tu espéreras, *etc.*

Verbs ending in **yer** generally change the *y* into *i* before an *e* mute ; as,

to pay **payer**

I pay *je paie* or *paye*	I shall pay *je paierai*
we pay *nous payons*	or *je payerai*

18

FORMATION OF TENSES.

French Tenses are either *Primitive* or *Derivative*.

The *Primitive* Tenses—called *Primitive* because the others are derived from them—are . the *Infinitive*, the *Present Participle*, the *Past Participle*, the *Present* and the *Past Definite* of the *Indicative*.

1. From the *Present Infinitive* are formed
- The Future, by adding the endings of the Present Indicative of AVOIR · *ai, as, a, ons, ez, ont.*
- The Conditional, by adding the endings of the Imperfect of AVOIR . *ais, ais, ait, ions, iez, aient.*

Infinitive	*Future*	*Conditional.*
parler	je parlerai	je parlerais
vendr(e)	je vendrai	je vendrais
finir	je finirai	je finirais

2 From the *Present Participle* are formed
- The Plural of the Present Indicative, by changing ANT into *ons, ez, ent*
- The Imperfect Indicative, by changing ANT into *ais, ais. ait, ions, iez, aient.*
- The Present Subjunctive, by changing ANT into *e, es, e, ions, iez, ent.*

Pres. Part.	*Plur. of Pres. Ind.*	*Imperfect.*	*Pres. Subj.*
parlant	nous { parlons	je { parlais	je { parle
vendant	{ vendons	{ vendais	{ vende
finissant	{ finissons	{ finissais	{ finisse

3 From the *Past Participle* are formed All the Compound Tenses, with the help of the auxiliary verbs *avoir* and *être.*

j'ai parlé   il est vendu   nous avons fini

4. From the *Present Indicative* is formed The Imperative, by omitting the Pronouns *je, nous, vous*

vous parlez *Imp* · parlez !   nous finissons *Imp.*: finissons !

5. From the 2nd person singular of the *Past Definite* is formed
The Imperfect Subjunctive, by adding *se, ses, sions, siez, sent,* changing *s* into *t* for the third person singular, and putting a circumflex accent over the vowel preceding the *t.*

Past Def	tu parlas	tu vendis	tu finis
Imperf. Subj ·	je parlasse	je vendisse	je finisse

All Tenses are formed by adding the respective terminations to the *Stem*, except in the *Future* and *Conditional*, where the terminations are added to the *Infinitive*

The above is the way in which the Formation of Tenses is usually explained. This, however, is quite an optional arrangement, and we consider it much simpler to say :

Verbs in ir prefix iss to the termination in the following cases :
1. Present Participle; 2. Plural of the Present Indicative;
3. Imperfect; 4. Present of the Subjunctive.

TRANSLATION OF "TO" BEFORE A VERB.

The *second* of two *Verbs* coming together must be in the *Infinitive*; as,

I must **speak**, *je dois* **parler**.
he forgot to **write** to us, *il a oublié de nous* écrire

The Auxiliaries *avoir* and *être* are followed by the Past Participle.

"TO" before a Verb must be translated.

For example : *parler*, *finir*, do not mean to *speak*, to *finish*, but are simply the Infinitives *speak*, *finish*

The following are the various ways in which to has to be translated.

1. **To** *between two Verbs* is generally translated **de**, unless it means *in order to*, when it is rendered by *pour* ; as,

I advise you to speak to him, *je vous conseille de lui parler*.
We did it (in order) to please him, *nous l'avons fait* **pour** *lui plaire*.

TO (not meaning *in order to*) should therefore be translated DE, unless it comes after any of the Verbs in the following Lists, which are intended

FOR REFERENCE ONLY.

2. **To** is not translated at all after the following

VERBS REQUIRING NO PREPOSITION
before the next Verb

The most important are marked *

aimer mieux*	faillir	préférer
aller	faire*	regarder
assurer	falloir*	revenir
compter	s'imaginer	savoir
croire	laisser	sembler
daigner	mener	souhaiter
déclarer	nier	soutenir
désirer*	oser*	valoir mieux*
devoir*	paraître	venir*
entendre*	penser	voir*
envoyer	pouvoir*	voler
espérer	prétendre	vouloir*

EXAMPLES

He is **going to** sing, *il va chanter*.
Does he **dare to** come ? *ose-t-il venir* ?

Verbs of motion, such as *courir*, or denoting a sense such as *sentir*, also require no Preposition before the following *Infinitive*.

3. To is translated *à* if coming after one of the following
VERBS REQUIRING THE PREPOSITION "à"
before the next Verb.

s abaisser	consister	inviter*
aboutir	conspirer	se mettre
s'accorder	contribuer	montrer
accoutumer*	convier	s'obstiner
s'acharner	se décider	s'offrir
admettre	se destiner	pencher
s'adonner	déterminer	persister
aider*	se déterminer	se plier
aimer†	se dévouer	porter
s'amuser	se disposer	pousser
s'animer	employer	prendre plaisir
s'appliquer	encourager	préparer*
apprendre*	engager*	procéder
s'apprêter	enhardir	provoquer
aspirer	s enhardir	recommencer*
s'assujettir	s'entendre	réduire
s'attacher	être	se réduire
s'attendre	s'évertuer	se refuser
autoriser	exceller	renoncer*
avoir*	exciter	résigner
avoir peine	s'exercer	se résoudre
balancer	exhorter	réussir
borner	s'exposer	songer*
chercher	se fatiguer	soumettre
se complaire	se former	tendre
concourir	s'habituer	tenir
se condamner	se hasarder	travailler
condescendre	hésiter*	viser
consentir	intéresser	se vouer

EXAMPLES : he will not consent to do it, *il ne consentira pas* à *le faire*
I am endeavouring to understand you, *je cherche* à *vous comprendre.*

The *following Verbs* take either *à* or *de* before the following *Infinitive*, according to meaning or euphony ; *à*, however, is more usual.

VERBS REQUIRING "à" OR "de"
before the next Verb.

s'accoutumer	s'efforcer	se hasarder	répugner
aimer†	s'empresser	se lasser	servir
commencer	s'engager	manquer	souffrir
consentir	s'ennuyer	obliger	suffire
continuer	s'entêter	s'occuper	tâcher
contraindre	essayer	oublier	tarder
convier	forcer	plaire	se tuer
demander	s'habituer	prier	venir
déterminer	haïr	refuser	

†*aimer* is usually followed by *à*, or no Preposition, but occasionally by *de.*

The Student should note the following differences in meaning, according to whether *à* or *de* is used. The other differences are very slight and unimportant.

Plaire, répugner, servir, suffire, and *tarder* are followed by **de** when used impersonally, in other cases by **à** , as,

It pleases me to do that, *il me plaît de faire cela.*
Do not delay doing it, *ne tardez pas à le faire.*

Manquer à implies omission or neglect , as,

I have omitted to write to him, *j'ai manqué à lui écrire.*

Manquer de is used in the sense of "to nearly do a thing"; as,

He almost lost his life, *il a manqué de perdre la vie.*

S'empresser, "to be eager to," may be followed by **à** or **de.** When meaning "to hasten" it always takes **de.**

Venir à means "to chance, or happen to"; as,

If he happened to lose it, *s'il venait à le perdre.*

Venir de means "to have just" (see Idiomatic Tenses).

The following Verbs, which in English are followed by a Preposition before their *Object,* take *no Preposition* in French.

admettre, *to admit of*
aller chercher,* *to go for*
approuver, *to approve of*
attendre,* *to wait for*
chercher,* *to look for*
écouter * *to listen to*

envoyer chercher,* *to send for*
espérer, *to hope for*
fournir, *to supply with*
prier Dieu, *to pray to God*
regarder,* *to look at*
rencontrer, *to meet with*

EXAMPLES
I am waiting for my friend, *j'attends mon ami.*
Look at that man, *regardez cet homme*

————o.o————

The following Verbs, which in English are not followed by a Preposition before their *Object,* take *à*; as,

apprendre,* *to teach (any one)*
conseiller, *to advise*
convenir, *to suit*
dire,* *to tell (any one)*
enseigner,* *to teach*
nuire, *to hurt*
obéir,* *to obey*
ordonner, *to order*
pardonner,* *to forgive*
parvenir, *to attain, manage*

permettre, *to permit*
plaire,* *to please*
remédier, *to remedy*
renoncer, *to renounce*
résigner, *to resign*
résister, *to resist*
ressembler, *to resemble*
succéder, *to succeed, follow*
survivre, *to outlive*
toucher,† *to touch*

EXAMPLES.
The soldiers obey the officers, *les soldats obéissent* **aux** *officiers.*
Do not touch this picture, *ne touchez pas* **à** *ce tableau.*

† *Toucher* can also be used without a following Preposition.

THE PRESENT PARTICIPLE.

The *Present Participle* is *variable* in Gender and Number when used as an *Adjective*, but is *invariable* when followed by an *Object* ; as,

A charming girl, *une fille charmant*e
A girl charming everyone, *une fille* charmant *tout le monde.*

The *English Present Participle* used as a Noun is replaced in French by the *Infinitive*, or a *Noun* ; as,

Hunting is a great pleasure, la chasse *est un grand plaisir.*
Dancing is pleasant, danser *est agréable.*

All Prepositions except en are followed by the *Infinitive.*

without waiting, *sans* attendre
after having spoken, *après* avoir *parlé*
in reading, *en* lisant

THE PAST PARTICIPLE.

The *Past Participle* only agrees in Gender and Number with the Subject when the *Compound Tenses* are formed with *être*; as,

She has gone out, *elle est sorti*e.   Have they started? *Sont-ils partis?*

The *Past Participle* also agrees with a Direct Object which *precedes* it, unless used as an AUXILIARY; as,

I have seen her, *je l'ai vu*e
The pencils I wanted, *les crayons que j'ai voulu*s
The pencils I wanted to see, *les crayons que j'ai* voulu *voir.*

The *Past Participle* never agrees with an *Indirect* Object.

NOTE.—*Se* if not Accusative, and *en*, are INDIRECT OBJECTS.

EXAMPLES.

I have spoken to her. *je lui ai* parlé
She has broken her leg, *elle s'est* cassé *la jambe*
We have given him some of them, *nous lui en avons* donné

IMPERSONAL VERBS.

Impersonal Verbs have no person or thing as their subject, and are only used in the third person singular ; as,

it happens, *il arrive* ;   it matters, *il importe*
was it raining? *pleuvait-il?*   it has been necessary, *il a fallu*
there does not remain, *il ne reste pas*

Y avoir, "there ... to be," is formed by putting **y** before the Third Person Singular of *avoir* ; as,

there is,* *il y a* | there is not, *il n'y a pas*
is there? *y a-t-il?* | is there not? *n'y a-t-il pas?*
there will be, *il y aura* | would there not be? *n'y aurait-il pas,* etc.

† These expressions are also used for *there are, there were,* &c.

IDIOMATIC TENSES.

PRESENT.

I am going to		*je vais*	
thou art going to	speak	*tu vas*	*parler*
he is going to	*or*	*il va*	*or*
we are going to	write	*nous allons*	*écrire*
you are going to	*or*	*vous allez*	*or*
they are going to	finish	*ils vont*	*finir*

PAST.

I was going to		*j'allais*	
thou wast going to	speak	*tu allais*	*parler*
he was going to	*or*	*il allait*	*or*
we were going to	write	*nous allions*	*écrire*
you were going to	*or*	*vous alliez*	*or*
they were going to	finish	*ils allaient*	*finir*

PRESENT.

I have just		*je viens de (d')*	
thou hast just	spoken	*tu viens de*	*parler*
he has just	*or*	*il vient de*	*or*
we have just	written	*nous venons de*	*écrire*
you have just	*or*	*vous venez de*	*or*
they have just	finished	*ils viennent de*	*finir*

PAST.

I had just		*je venais de*	
thou hadst just	spoken	*tu venais de*	*parler*
he had just	*or*	*il venait de*	*or*
we had just	written	*nous venions de*	*ecrire*
you had just	*or*	*vous veniez de*	*or*
they had just	finished	*ils venaient de*	*finir*

PRESENT.

I am to		*je dois*	
thou art to	speak	*tu dois*	*parler*
he is to	*or*	*il doit*	*or*
we are to	write	*nous devons*	*écrire*
you are to	*or*	*vous devez*	*or*
they are to	finish	*ils doivent*	*finir*

PAST.

I was to speak, etc	*je devais parler,* etc.
I ought to speak, etc.	*je devrais parler,* etc.
I ought to have spoken, etc.	*j'aurais dû parler,* etc.

The following is a Model of the Principal Tenses of an English Verb The Names of the Tenses are those which are generally made use of in the Conjugation of Foreign Verbs.

It is very important to know what English words are represented by the names *Present, Imperfect, Future*, etc For example. *I am calling* is just as much *Present* as *I call*, and *I shall be calling* and *I shall call* are both *Future*.

Notice particularly the Auxiliaries used in the Conjugation of *Future* and *Conditional* in English.

INFINITIVE: to call

PRESENT PARTICIPLE. calling   PAST PARTICIPLE called

PRESENT TENSE		IMPERFECT *or* PAST.	
I call	*or* I am	I called	*or* I was
thou callest	*or* thou art	thou calledst	*or* thou wast
he calls	*or* he is ⟩ calling	he called	*or* he is ⟩ calling
we call	*or* we are	we called	*or* we were
you call	*or* you are	you called	*or* you were
they call	*or* they are	they called	*or* they were

FUTURE.

I shall		I shall be	
thou wilt		thou wilt be	
he will	⟩ call *or*	he will be	⟩ calling
we shall		we shall be	
you will		you will be	
they will		they will be	

CONDITIONAL.

I should		I should be	
thou wouldst		thou wouldst be	
he would	⟩ call *or*	he would be	⟩ calling
we should		we should be	
you would		you would be	
they would		they would be	

IMPERATIVE.

call, let him call. let us call, let them call.

PERFECT.

I have		I have been	
thou hast		thou hast been	
he has	⟩ called *or*	he has been	⟩ calling
we have		we have been	
you have		you have been	
they have		they have been	

PLUPERFECT.

I had		I had been	
thou hadst		thou hadst been	
he had	⟩ called *or*	he had been	⟩ calling
we had		we had been	
you had		you had been	
they had		they had been	

FUTURE PERFECT

I shall have called, etc. *or* I shall have been calling, etc.

CONDITIONAL PERFECT.

I should have called, etc. *or* I should have been calling, etc

HUGO'S
French Conversation Simplified

In Three Sections.—I. Simple Sentences with Pronunciation. II. Easy Conversation, with Explanatory Notes. III. Conversation of Medium Difficulty.

This work is indeed a ROYAL ROAD TO TALKING FRENCH. No one who has mastered the first section can ever be at a loss to express his meaning in good simple French. This can be accomplished in a few weeks by anyone with a fair knowledge of French grammar who works an hour or two a day, on the plan laid down in the preface. In the First Section, the

PRONUNCIATION OF EVERY SENTENCE IS IMITATED.

256 pages, strongly bound in cloth ... **4/6** net.

HUGO'S
French Reading Simplified

Contents : Novelettes, Poetry, Extracts from standard writers and modern periodicals, Amusing Anecdotes and Dialogues, with Interesting and Instructive Paragraphs from various sources, carefully selected and fully annotated.

20,000 EXPLANATORY FOOT-NOTES.	NO DICTIONARY REQUIRED.

Complete in one volume, 384 pages, cloth ... **5/-** net.

HUGO'S
French Composition Made Easy

Contents : Connected Conversations, Anecdotes, Commercial Phrases, etc., carefully graduated and fully annotated, so that translation into French of NATURAL COLLOQUIAL ENGLISH becomes quite easy after a few weeks' work.

THE ONLY PRACTICAL AND PRACTICABLE WORK OF THE KIND EVER PUBLISHED.

A striking contrast to the untranslatable high-flown matter given in the average composition book.

212 pages, complete with KEY, **5/-** net.

Lightning Source UK Ltd.
Milton Keynes UK
UKOW05f1501030616

275535UK00008B/127/P